Collections Times Four

by Emma Magirescu

HOUGHTON MIFFLIN   BOSTON

PHOTOGRAPHY CREDITS
Cover © PhotoDisc, © Comstock, © HMCo./Sharon Hoogstraten Photography; **1** © HMCo./Sharon Hoogstraten Photography; **2–4** © HMCo./Sharon Hoogstraten Photography; **6–7** © HMCo./Sharon Hoogstraten Photography; **8** © Digital Vision; **9** © Comstock; © Corbis; © PhotoDisc; **10** © Photodisc; **11** ©HMCo./Sharon Hoogstraten Photography

Printed in China

ISBN 13: 978-0-618-89968-5
ISBN 10: 0-618-89968-5

19 20 21 22 23 24 0940 21 20 19 18 17 16

4500607556

Collecting objects can be fun. You can collect almost anything. My name is Karen and I collect rocks and gemstones. There are four people in my family, and everyone collects something.

When your collection gets big, sometimes it's hard to keep track of how many things you've collected.

turquiose pyrite quartz tiger eye

My rock collection has many different kinds of rocks, but my four favorite kinds are pyrite, turquoise, tiger eye, and quartz. I have four of each kind.

If I want to know how many of my favorite rocks I have, I could draw a picture of the four kinds of rocks and add them together.

I have four of each kind. There are four groups, and each group contains four rocks.

$$4 + 4 + 4 + 4 = \underline{\quad}$$

Read·Think·Write How many of her favorite rocks are in Karen's collection?

4

My dad collects coins. He started his collection when he was just a boy, and he is still collecting them. My favorite part of his collection is the silver dollars. He has three columns of sliver dollars.

It's easy to see how many silver dollars Dad has if I count the columns. There are four silver dollars in each of the three columns.

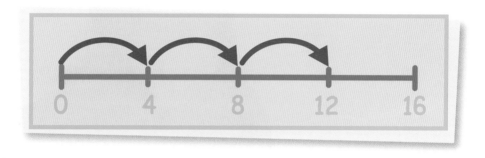

Read·Think·Write How many silver dollars does Karen's dad have?

Mom takes photographs and collects the best ones. She started by collecting our baby photos. Now, she collects vacation photos, photos of scenery, and photos of special events.

Mom has chosen some of her photos to enter in a show. She has chosen five baby photos and five vacation photos.

$$I \text{ know } 2 \times 5 = 10.$$

Mom has also chosen five photos of scenery and five photos of special events.

It's easy to see how many photos Mom has chosen.

$$\text{If } 2 \times 5 = 10$$
$$\text{Then,}$$
$$10 \times 2 = ?$$

Read·Think·Write How many photos has Karen's mom chosen in all?

My little brother, Jeffrey, has a collection too.
His collection is a little bit different. He likes
to collect rubber ducks! Some are large and some
are small.

Jeffrey has just started his collection. He likes to put them in rows.

He says they are swimming in line, but it makes them easy to count and multiply. He has two groups of four ducks.

$$2 \times 4 = ?$$

Read·Think·Write How many ducks does Jeffery have?

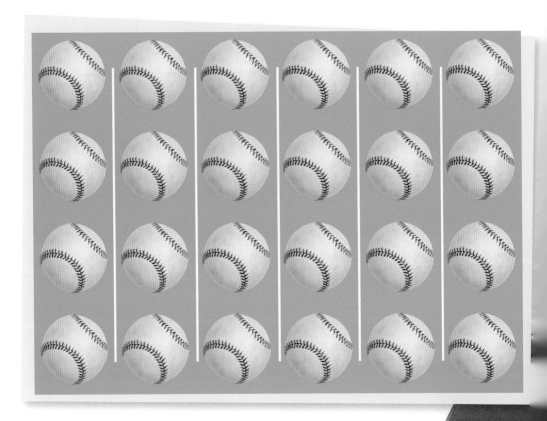

So if you want to know how many objects are in your collection, you can multiply four ways. You can draw a picture and use repeated addition, skip-count, double the product, or write a multiplication sentence.

Read·Think·Write How many baseballs are in this collection?

There are four people in my family and we each have a collection. We collect rocks, coins, photos, and rubber ducks.

Read·Think·Write What do you collect?

1. Draw Conclusions Karen has added four amethysts to her collection. Draw a picture and use repeated addition to find out how many rocks she has in total.

2. What is a multiplication sentence to show how many silver dollars Dad has collected?

3. Use the skip-counting strategy to find out how many photos Mom has chosen.

4. If you multiplied Jeffrey's 8 rubber ducks times 2, what would the product be? Use double the double strategy.

Activity

Use a collection of 20 items and put them into equal groups.

What are the two multiplication sentences you can write for your groups?